THE AMAZING HUMAN BODY

Pump It Up
The Heart and Blood

Edited by
Joanne Randolph

Enslow Publishing
101 W. 23rd Street
Suite 240
New York, NY 10011
USA
enslow.com

This edition published in 2018 by:
Enslow Publishing, LLC.
101 W. 23rd Street, Suite 240
New York, NY 10011

Library of Congress Cataloging-in-Publication Data

Names: Randolph, Joanne, editor.
Title: Pump it up : the heart and blood / edited by Joanne Randolph.
Description: New York, NY : Enslow Publishing, 2018. | Series: The amazing human body | Includes bibliographical references and index.
Identifiers: LCCN 2017001868 | ISBN 9780766089877 (library bound book) | ISBN 9780766089853 (pbk. book) | ISBN 9780766089860 (6 pack)
Subjects: LCSH: Blood—Circulation—Juvenile literature. | Heart—Juvenile literature. | Cardiovascular system—Juvenile literature.
Classification: LCC QP103 .P86 2018 | DDC 612.1/1—dc23
LC record available at https://lccn.loc.gov/2017001868

Printed in China

To Our Readers: We have done our best to make sure all website addresses in this book were active and appropriate when we went to press. However, the author and the publisher have no control over and assume no liability for the material available on those websites or on any websites they may link to. Any comments or suggestions can be sent by email to customerservice@enslow.com.

CONTENTS

CHAPTER 1

Nonstop Pumping 4

CHAPTER 2

Oxygen and a Dangerous Competitor 17

CHAPTER 3

A Day in the Life of Blood 28

CHAPTER 4

Blood: There Is No Substitute 35

Glossary 46
Further Reading 47
Index 48

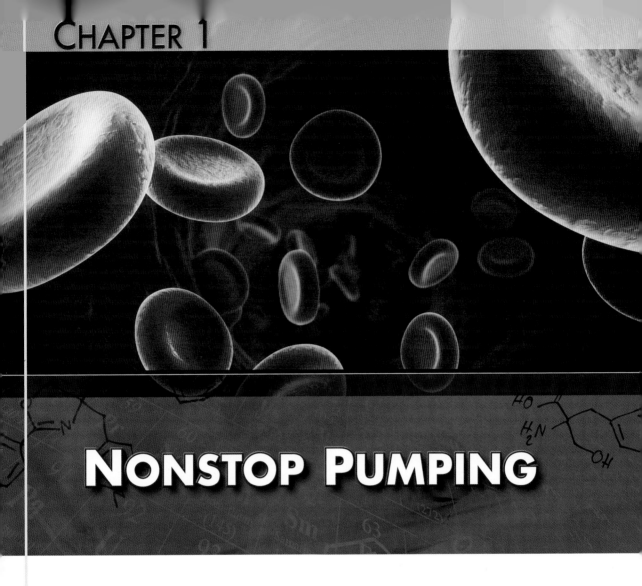

NONSTOP PUMPING

S hine a flashlight in your mouth. That red glow in your cheek is your blood, the liquid of life.

Try this: press two fingers gently against the side of your neck, below your chin. Feel the little thump-thump? That's your heart pumping blood through your veins. The heart and the veins make up your circulatory, or cardiovascular, system.

THE HEART

The human heart is the pumping station of the circulatory system. It pushes blood through the body's blood vessels. The heart is divided into four chambers. The top two chambers are the left and right atria. Blood enters the heart through the atria. It is then pushed back out through the two bottom chambers, called the left and right ventricles. The chambers are separated by valves that open and close as the heart beats. There are other valves that control the flow of blood from the arteries and the veins.

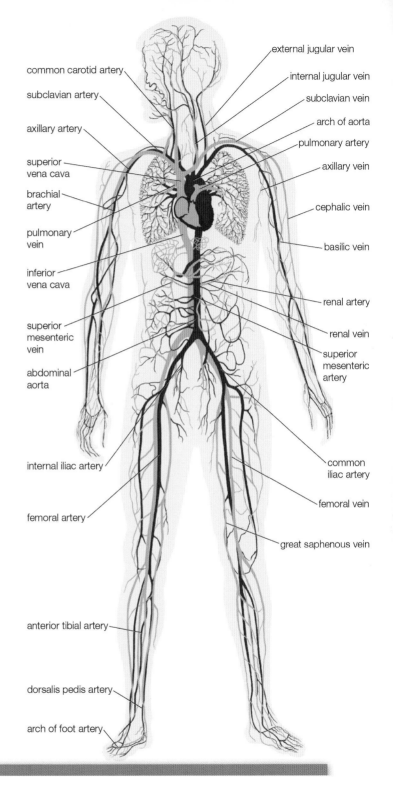

common carotid artery

subclavian artery

axillary artery

superior vena cava

brachial artery

pulmonary vein

inferior vena cava

superior mesenteric vein

abdominal aorta

internal iliac artery

femoral artery

anterior tibial artery

dorsalis pedis artery

arch of foot artery

external jugular vein

internal jugular vein

subclavian vein

arch of aorta

pulmonary artery

axillary vein

cephalic vein

basilic vein

renal artery

renal vein

superior mesenteric artery

common iliac artery

femoral vein

great saphenous vein

This image shows the cardiovascular system. Each trip the blood makes from heart to toes and back again requires about twenty seconds.

THE BLOOD

Your blood is always on the move. Once every minute, it travels all the way around your body and back again to your heart.

Your heart pumps all that blood around. Today, every school kid knows that. But for thousands of years, even the greatest doctors in the world didn't know why the heart beat or what flowed through the body's many tubes. (Some thought veins also carried air or even your spirit.) What goes on inside the human body was just as mysterious as the stars.

GLADIATOR SCHOOL

That's really not too surprising, once you stop to think about it. After all, you can't see through your skin. You can feel some of the things that are going on inside you—you can feel your heart beating, or your chest filling with air. You can listen to the weird gurgling in your stomach. You can see that food and water go in one end of you and come out the other. But what goes on in-between? With no way to look inside, doctors could only guess.

Of course, even in ancient times, when people butchered animals for food or got injured in battles, they could see organs and blood. But it wasn't always easy to figure out how all that messy stuff works inside a living person.

One of the earliest doctors to investigate what goes on in the body was a Greek called Galen (130–200 CE). Galen got his start tending to wounded gladiators, professional fighters who fought with real weapons in front of cheering crowds. As you might expect, gladiators did a lot of bleeding. Perhaps this inspired Galen's interest

Galen mainly relied on animals to study the inner workings of the body. This meant his findings did not always apply to humans. But he was the first to use the pulse as a tool in measuring health, which is still done today.

in blood. It certainly gave him a good way to study the insides of bodies. Galen also carefully cut open dead animals to discover how they work. The books Galen wrote were used by doctors for hundreds of years.

Unfortunately, many of Galen's ideas were totally wrong. For instance, Galen didn't know that the heart beats because it is pumping blood. He thought that blood vessels pulsed on their own, pulling blood into the heart. He also had no idea that the same blood circulates over and over again through the body. He thought that blood got used up as soon as it left the heart and that the liver constantly made new blood from the food we eat.

According to Galen, inside the heart, dark blood made from digested food in the liver was warmed, and a life-giving substance called "vital spirit" was added to it. Galen believed that the lungs made this vital spirit out of air, and that it turned the blood bright red. Well, he was right that blood gets something from the air. . . .

THE CIRCLE OF BLOOD

Galen's views were unquestioned for almost 1,500 years. In fact, doctors who doubted Galen were sometimes burned at the stake. It wasn't until the 1600s that an English doctor named William Harvey figured out that the heart pumps blood around the body.

Simple math told Harvey that Galen couldn't be right that each heartbeat pumped all-new blood. Harvey measured the blood pumped out by each beat of the heart: about 2 ounces (59 milliliters). That means that a heart beating seventy-two times a minute pushes out 9 pounds (4 kilograms) of blood. For Galen to

Here, William Harvey shows King Charles I his theory on how the circulation of blood works.

be right, a person's liver would need to be making 540 pounds (245 kg) of blood every hour from the food a person ate. It couldn't be done! The answer had to be that the same blood is pumped over and over again. As Harvey put it: "I began to think there was some sort of motion as in a circle."

By doing simple experiments that involved pinching off arteries and veins, Harvey was able to map the blood flow through the heart and around the body. The right side of the heart pumps blood to the lungs; the blood then returns to the left side of the heart, where it is pumped to the rest of the body.

ARTERY AND VEIN

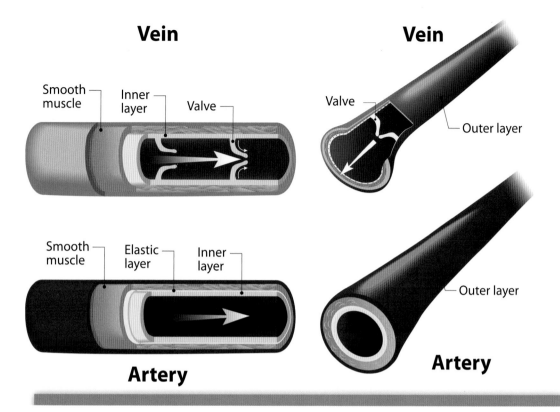

This cross-section of a vein and an artery lets us see the valves in the veins that direct and control the flow of blood.

Harvey's first clue that blood circulates around and around was the discovery of tiny flaps like little doors in medium and large veins. Harvey noticed that the doors, called valves, only open in one direction, which helps keep the blood flowing toward the heart and against the pull of gravity. (Otherwise, there would be backflow and pooling, especially in the arms and legs). Because of these valves, the blood in each vein can only flow one way—around the body in a big loop. Arteries do not have valves; the pressure created by the heart pumping is high enough to prevent the backflow of blood.

WHAT IS BLOOD?

Harvey didn't get everything right. He didn't know exactly why blood circulates. He thought, for instance, that blood traveled to the lungs to be cooled. Today we know that blood picks up oxygen in the lungs (and gets rid of carbon dioxide).

And it does much more. Blood carries food, minerals, germ fighters, and chemical messages all over the body. It also collects waste chemicals from cells. The liver and kidneys filter out the wastes and send them to be expelled in pee and poop.

Blood is made up of several different kinds of cells floating in a yellowish liquid called plasma. A 100-pound (45 kg) person has about 7 pounds (3 kg) of blood in his or her body. Every drop contains millions of cells.

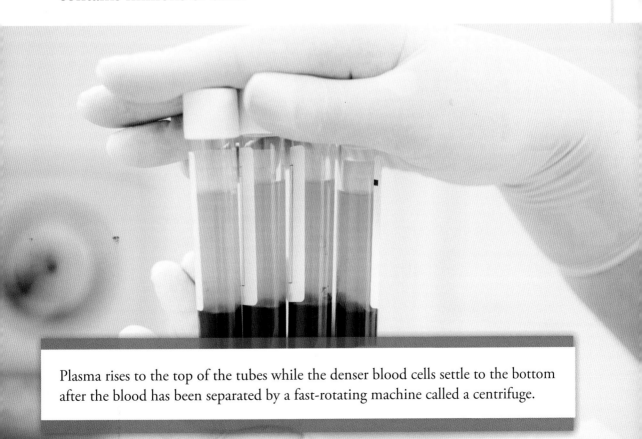

Plasma rises to the top of the tubes while the denser blood cells settle to the bottom after the blood has been separated by a fast-rotating machine called a centrifuge.

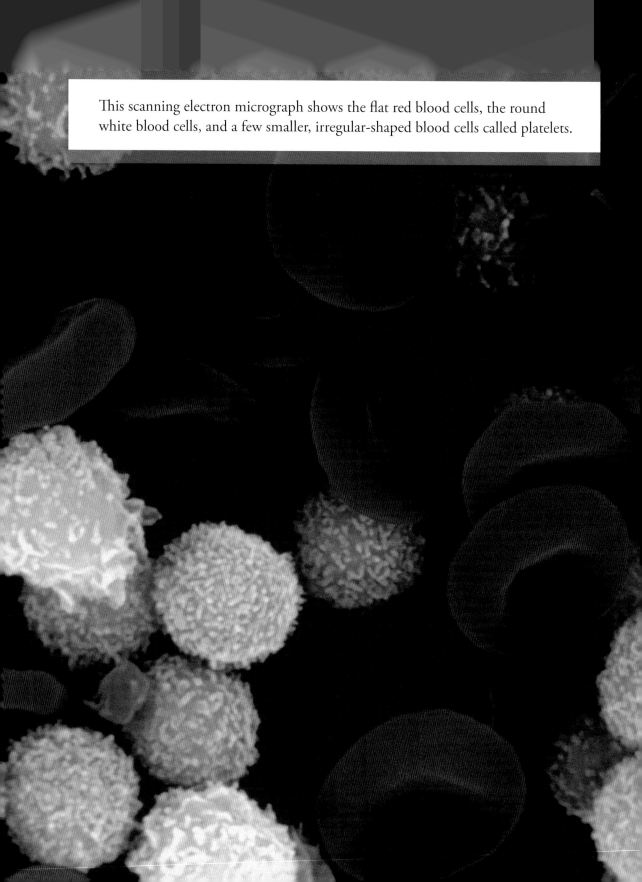

This scanning electron micrograph shows the flat red blood cells, the round white blood cells, and a few smaller, irregular-shaped blood cells called platelets.

Each blood cell has a job to do. Red blood cells carry oxygen from the lungs to the rest of the body. White blood cells are the defense team. They fight bacteria and viruses that cause disease. Platelets are the repair crew. They float around in the blood but get spiky and stick together if a blood vessel is damaged. This makes a clot, a little plug to stop the bleeding.

Red blood cells are filled with hemoglobin, a special oxygen-trapping molecule. The hemoglobin snags oxygen at the lungs and lets go of it at cells. Hemoglobin is red, and it gives blood its red color.

Each red blood cell lasts about four months. In that time it will make about seventy-five thousand trips around your body. When blood cells wear out, marrow inside your bones makes new blood cells to replace them.

Every second of every day, your heart beats. Thump thump! Although only the size of your fist, your heart is the most powerful muscle in your body. That's because it has the most important job—to keep the blood flowing, around and around.

THE BODY'S DELIVERY SYSTEM

The first job of blood is to pick up oxygen from the lungs and carry it to every cell in the body. Arteries flow away from the heart. They carry bright red blood filled with oxygen. Your cells need oxygen to release stored energy. The blood also picks up the waste product of oxygen, carbon dioxide, and the veins bring it to the lungs to be expelled from the body. The liver filters the blood and checks to make sure the blood has the right chemical balance. If the mix isn't quite right, the liver tries to fix it. Meanwhile, your two kidneys remove wastes from the blood and mix them with extra water to make pee. Your bladder stores the liquid waste until you can get rid of it.

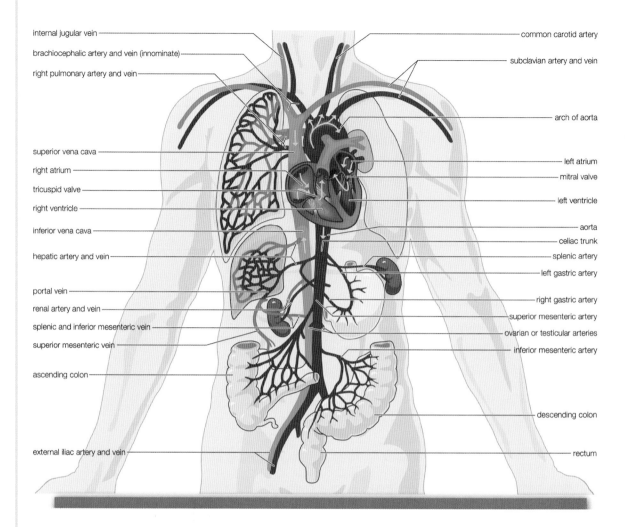

internal jugular vein
brachiocephalic artery and vein (innominate)
right pulmonary artery and vein
superior vena cava
right atrium
tricuspid valve
right ventricle
inferior vena cava
hepatic artery and vein
portal vein
renal artery and vein
splenic and inferior mesenteric vein
superior mesenteric vein
ascending colon
external iliac artery and vein

common carotid artery
subclavian artery and vein
arch of aorta
left atrium
mitral valve
left ventricle
aorta
celiac trunk
splenic artery
left gastric artery
right gastric artery
superior mesenteric artery
ovarian or testicular arteries
inferior mesenteric artery
descending colon
rectum

This diagram shows how the veins and arteries bring blood
to and from the body's organs and limbs.

Blood also carries a constant stream of chemical messages
between the brain and different body parts. This helps all the organs
work together. Blood also moves heat around, keeping your whole
body at the same temperature.

Blood vessels seem to be everywhere in the body. All these tubes
carry blood to every part of your body, even inside bones. The only

place they don't go is inside your brain. Blood circulates around the brain and drops off its oxygen and sugars, but it doesn't go inside.

IS MY FACE RED?

Eager to get that last bit of ice cream soda, you slurp hard... SRRRWRRT. Everyone in the restaurant turns around to stare. Oops! If you're like many people, your face has just gone bright red. Why?

Blushing is an automatic response that happens when you're embarrassed. When you make a social goof (or think you might

Blushing can happen when a person is angry, as well as when he or she is embarrassed. These emotions cause adrenaline to be released into your bloodstream, which in turn dilates the veins in your face, allowing more blood to enter your cheeks.

have), a small gland in your middle makes adrenaline, a fear chemical that wakes you up. Adrenaline also widens blood vessels in your face, letting in more blood—and giving your cheeks that unmistakable hot pink flush.

Humans are the only animals that blush. Scientists still aren't entirely sure why we do it. But it might have evolved as a way to signal to others that we know we've made a misstep—an automatic "Sorry!" that can't be faked.

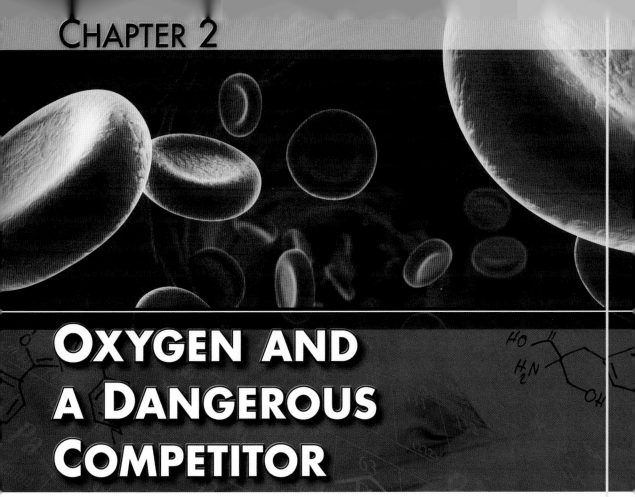

CHAPTER 2

OXYGEN AND A DANGEROUS COMPETITOR

Every second, stem cells in your bone marrow give birth to about two million red blood cells. These baby cells have one main mission: picking up and delivering oxygen. Once they begin to work, they never rest. But first, each cell must prepare itself. Remaining in the bone marrow, and under the orders of the DNA in its nucleus, the cell spends its first week manufacturing hemoglobin. Once stuffed with millions of these red protein molecules, the baby cell jettisons its nucleus and all protein-making machinery. Now mature, the red cell is one of the tiniest cells in the body—a flattened, flexible disc able to penetrate the deepest recesses of every organ. Ready for work as an oxygen ferry, it plunges into the bloodstream.

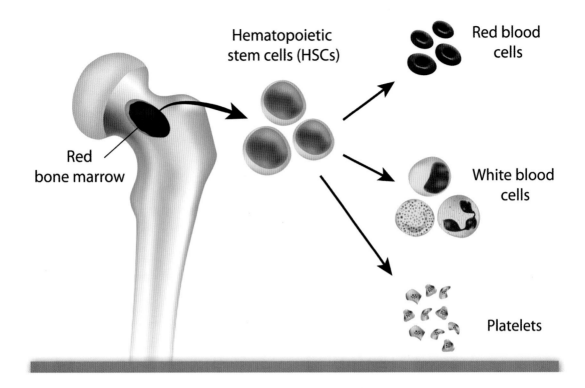

Hematopoietic stem cells (HSCs)

Red blood cells

White blood cells

Red bone marrow

Platelets

This diagram shows how the stem cells create the different blood cells.

A CONTINUOUS JOURNEY: SEATBELTS REQUIRED

Each trip the red cell makes from heart and lungs to toes and back takes about twenty seconds. The passage begins in high-pressure, turbulent arteries and ends in the low-pressure, placid veins (carrying blood to the heart). In between the arteries and veins, red cells fall into single file, bending and twisting themselves through the smallest channels of all—the capillaries. Capillaries are boarding and disembarking stations for oxygen. Want to see blood flow through a capillary network? Put pressure on your fingertip until it turns white. Then let up and watch. That line of returning pink color is blood advancing through skin capillaries.

The red blood cells are shaped like a flattened donut so they can fold and flex enough to fit through tiny places such as capillaries.

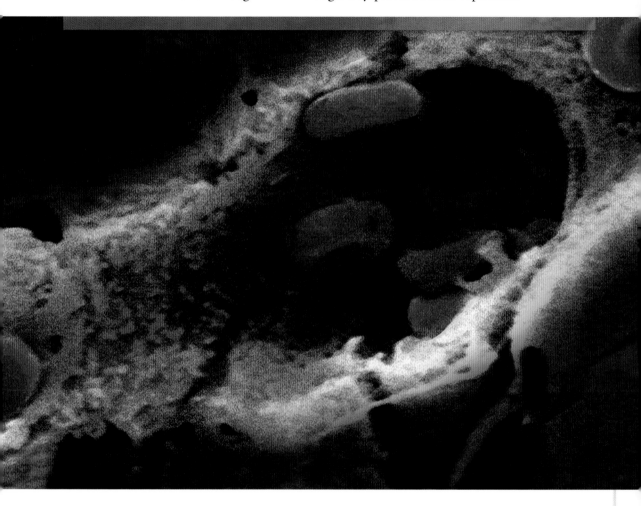

Each red cell is like an orderly passenger ferry. Millions of hemoglobin molecules line the interior, each with four seats for oxygen. Each seat is called a heme ring, with a molecule of iron at its center. Oxygen attaches itself to iron. Proteins called globins surround the heme rings—thus, the name hemoglobin. Hemoglobin must be able to attract oxygen and also to release it at the right time, which is fancy chemistry. The trick requires a molecular seatbelt system.

HEMOGLOBIN

Iron

Heme

Polypeptide
chain

Oxygen
molecules

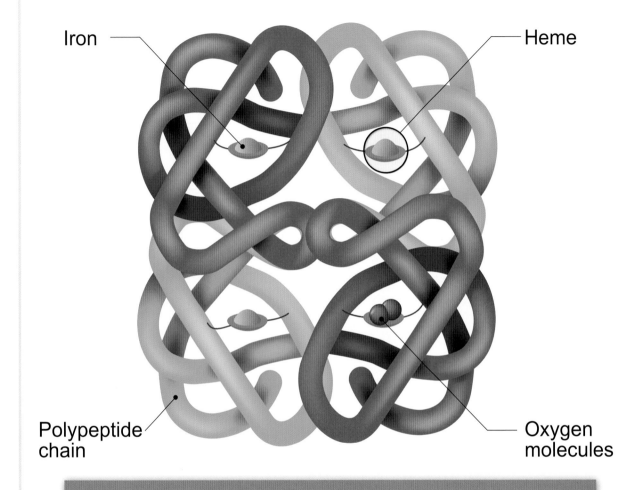

This diagram shows the structure of a hemoglobin molecule.
You can see the heme rings and the iron within it. In the
bottom corner, you can see the oxygen bonding to the iron.

Like a seatbelt, an arm of the hemoglobin molecule folds over
oxygen as soon as it settles into its iron seat in a red cell passing
through a lung capillary. Once closed, the seatbelt changes the shape
of hemoglobin, making blood a brighter red as it exits the lung

capillaries. As soon as the blood reaches the capillary networks of the body, it picks up carbon dioxide waste, which changes the blood chemistry. Carbon dioxide dissolves in blood and makes carbonic acid. Acidity pops the hemoglobin seatbelts open, and oxygen drifts out of the red cell, ready to burn for energy production. The more acidic the environment, such as in a hard-working muscle, the more oxygen hemoglobin gives up. Darker red now, blood returns to the lungs. Carbonic acid becomes carbon dioxide and disappears in your next exhaled breath. In the less acidic blood, seatbelts clamp down on new oxygen passengers for the next trip.

DANGER!

Until human beings started using fire, oxygen had little competition for the iron seats on the red cell ferry. But along with cooking food, heating houses, driving, boating, and smoking came carbon monoxide. Carbon monoxide is an odorless, tasteless gas produced whenever carbon-containing fuels burn. Like oxygen, carbon monoxide crosses from air into lung capillaries. It makes a bee-line for the iron seats, beating out oxygen two hundred times to one. Unlike oxygen it is very reluctant to give up its seat. And if that weren't bad enough, it makes the oxygen that does get on board reluctant to disembark. Oxygen shortage causes power failure in all kinds of cells.

Some warning symptoms of cellular power failure from carbon monoxide poisoning seem like the flu—fatigue, achy pain, headaches. Increasing blood levels of carbon monoxide cause shortness of breath, confusion, poor coordination, hallucinations, and finally stupor, coma, and death. Symptoms depend on how much carbon monoxide is in the air, how long someone breathes it in, and how healthy they are to begin with. Smokers carry some carbon monoxide in their blood all the time—not enough for noticeable symptoms, but enough to contribute to the poor health they gradually develop. Fumes from heat sources and engines running in closed spaces are the biggest culprits in acute poisoning, which requires time and breathing 100 percent oxygen to reverse.

All fires, engines, and appliances need to send their visible smoke and invisible gases outside, and they need to be checked for leaks regularly. Carbon monoxide detectors—especially where people sleep—are a very good idea. Any suspicion of carbon monoxide should make you and everyone else, including pets, get out into fresh air!

During the winter, people should always make sure their cars' exhaust pipes aren't blocked by snow. Otherwise, fumes may build up as the occupants warm up their cars and result in accidental carbon monoxide poisoning.

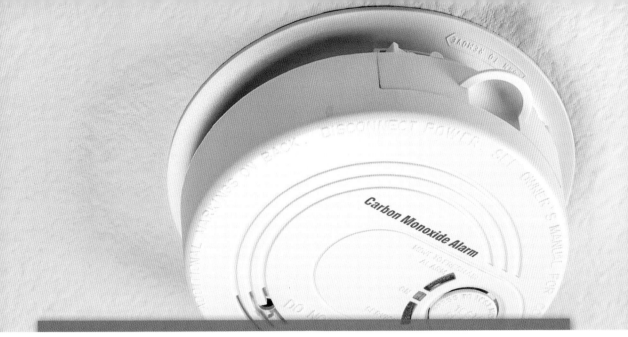

A carbon monoxide detector measures the amount of carbon monoxide in the environment over time. An alarm would go off before the gas reaches dangerous levels so people have enough time to save themselves.

Believe it or not, you are also a source of carbon monoxide, because you, too, burn carbon-based fuels for energy. Your carbon monoxide comes from recycling red blood cells. By the time red blood cells are 100 to 120 days old, they are decrepit, with tired, stiff membranes. Recyclers, especially in the liver and spleen, pull the old-timers out of the bloodstream and strip them for parts. Some parts get reused for different cells, but the heme ring is broken down for disposal. Part goes back to the lungs as carbon monoxide and gets exhaled. Part goes into the making of bile, the green liquid squirted out of the gall bladder into the intestines to aid in digestion of food. (Broken-down hemoglobin changes color, as you can easily see in a big bruise that turns eggplant purple, then green, then yellow.) Iron from the heme ring goes back to the bone marrow for reassembly into hemoglobin, keeping the supply lines stocked for those millions of baby cells your bone marrow keeps churning out.

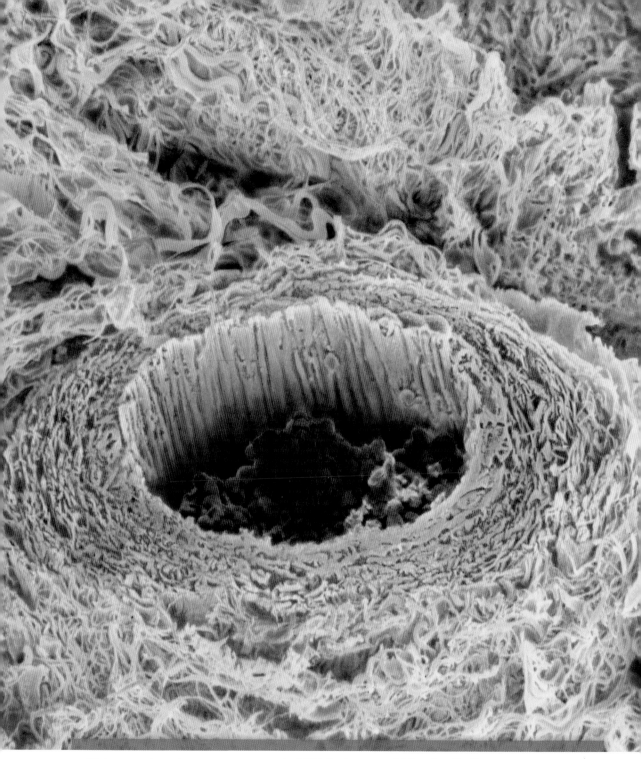

This scanning electron micrograph (SEM) shows red blood cells flowing through an arteriole, a small, terminal branch of an artery that leads into the capillaries. The red blood cells are red here because they have picked up oxygen from the lungs.

SICKLE CELL DISEASE – A "GLOBIN" PROBLEM

Globins are the globular-shaped proteins surrounding each of the four heme portions of the hemoglobin complex. Each hemoglobin molecule has two types of globin molecules, and together, they hold the whole structure together and keep the heme molecules oriented properly in space. While most people have the same kinds of globins, some people inherit slightly different ones. Most cause no major trouble. About one in eight children of African descent inherit a gene called sickle cell trait. Some scientists think sickle cell trait is common in people of African descent because it arose in a part of the world where malaria is common. The trait offers some

This diagram shows how sickle cells are not flexible like normal blood cells. Sickle cells can stick to the walls of blood vessels and block blood flow to tissues, causing pain and damage.

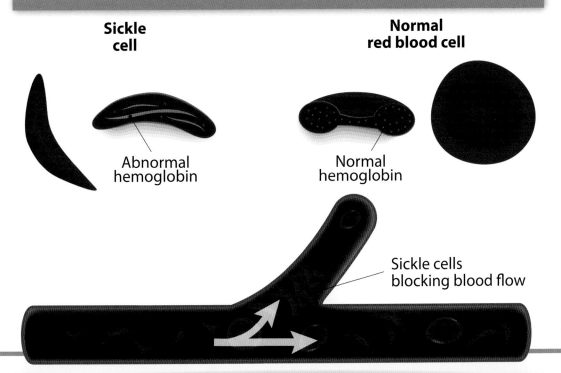

Sickle cell

Abnormal hemoglobin

Normal red blood cell

Normal hemoglobin

Sickle cells blocking blood flow

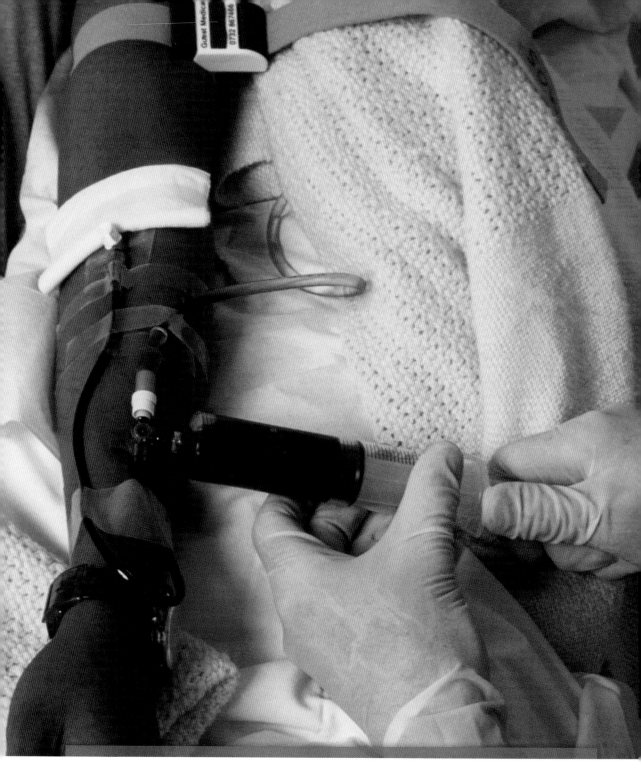

A patient with sickle-cell anemia receives a blood transfusion as treatment.

protection against malaria. But two copies of the gene, inherited by as many as one in five hundred children of African descent, produce hemoglobin that deforms red blood cells when they are not carrying oxygen. These sickle-shaped red blood cells stick to each other and clog small blood vessels, producing painful "crises" and damaging tissues. These children have sickle cell disease, and they require careful medical care over their whole lives.

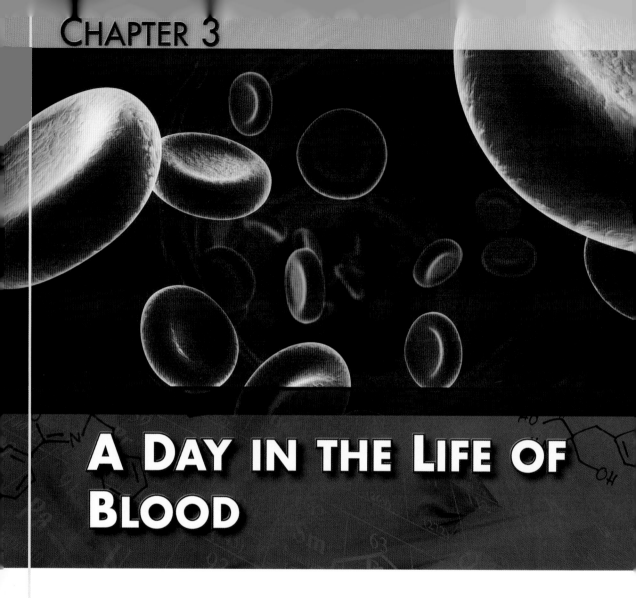

CHAPTER 3

A DAY IN THE LIFE OF BLOOD

Your body is home to a network of tunnels 62,137 miles (100,000 kilometers) long—long enough to stretch around Earth twice. These blood vessels range in thickness from about an inch (25 millimeters, a little bigger around than a nickel) to only 8 micrometers—1/100th the width of a hair or just thick enough to allow a single blood cell to pass at a time.

Through those blood vessel tunnels, the thick and the thin, travels your body's conveyor system, your blood. The list of blood

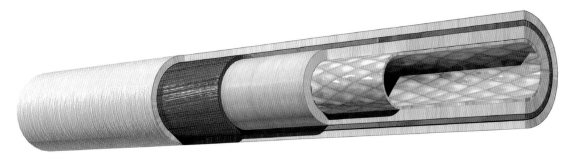

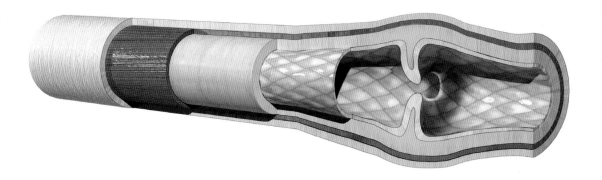

This diagram shows the differences between arteries (*top*), capillaries (*middle*), and veins (*bottom*). Do you see how small the capillaries are? They have fewer layers than the other two blood vessels, too.

functions is a list of life itself. The blood is vital for breathing, eating, fighting disease, disposing of waste, and regulating temperature. It's a system that heals itself, fuels itself, builds itself, and disposes of itself, all without a moment's conscious thought. All this happens even though the amount of blood in your body at one time is no more than four liters, barely more than would fill a gallon milk jug in your refrigerator. But blood isn't actually a liquid. It isn't a solid either. Instead, it is a plasma—a mixture of straw-colored fluid, dissolved chemicals, and suspended bodies: red cells, white cells, and platelets. Each plays a crucial role in keeping you alive.

A DANGEROUS WORLD

The world is full of danger. Today the danger is the knife you're using to slice an orange for an after-school snack. That sharp metal knife is great for cutting through rind and pulpy flesh, but your fingers are very near that razor edge.

Inside your network of tunnels, blood goes about its business. Your fingers are energized by the flow of oxygen-rich blood from

Blood is doing its job, no matter what you are working on. Your fingers have the oxygen and energy they need to chop vegetables or to comb your hair because of the blood.

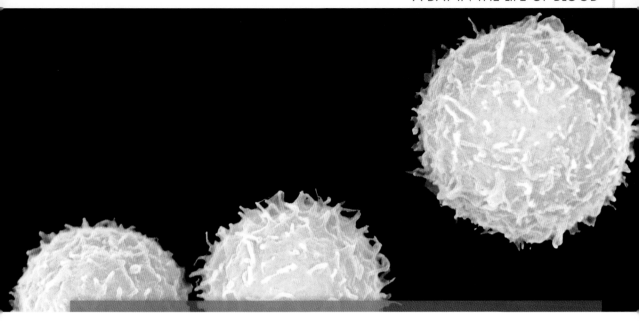

There are different kinds of white blood cells that specialize in different targets, such as disease, fungi, allergens, and other intruders.

your lungs. Red cells release their store of oxygen inside the tiniest of your tunnels, the capillaries. At the same time, energy-rich glucose passes from the plasma into your fingers' millions of cells. There, glucose and oxygen combine to release the energy your fingers need to stay warm, to move, to live. In exchange for this energy-rich supply, your finger cells dump into your blood the ash of life— carbon dioxide and other waste chemicals—that your blood will move along to their final destinations.

Alongside the red cells swim a whole zoo of white blood cells. These expert disease-fighters all have their own special jobs and their own set of villains for which they're constantly on the lookout. Vastly outnumbered by the red blood cells, the white cells keep silent watch, ensuring that all is well.

But these are not the cells of interest today. For at this very moment (ouch!) the knife slips, a finger is cut, and a vessel begins to leak.

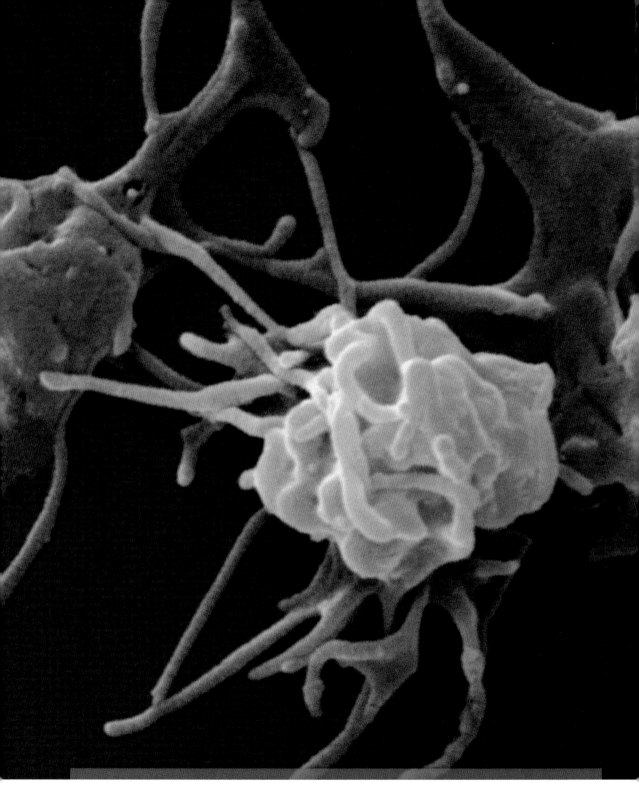

Activated platelets work to stop bleeding in the body.

EMERGENCY!

With only about a gallon of blood coursing through all those thousands of miles of tunnels, even a small leak is an immediate problem. But the blood is ready. Riding to the rescue are the platelets, the smallest components of the blood. Platelets are not proper cells; they're more like pieces of cells, broken off from their mother cell (called a megakaryocyte) for one specific purpose.

Now the platelets are on the move. Wherever in the body a cut might occur, the platelets slide in to stanch the flow. This cut is clean; the blood is pushing through. The platelets throw themselves into the wound, and soon the flow slows to a trickle.

The platelets aren't just flow-blockers. Instead, as they adhere to the edges of the cut, they release chemical signals that call for backup. It soon arrives in the form of a protein called fibrin. As you might guess from the name, fibrin builds a connective, fibrous web that binds the platelets together and closes the wound.

DANGER FROM WITHIN

Cuts are dangerous, but the body's own defenses can be dangerous, too. The elements to make a clot are always present in the blood. Scientists say that just two milliliters of blood hold enough clotting elements to freeze the body's entire circulatory system. These high-octane chemicals must be kept in check, to avoid unwanted clots.

On the other hand, if even one of these chemicals is missing, the body might not be able to stop even the most minor of leaks. Hemophilia is a condition in which even the smallest cut continues to bleed. It occurs when one of the chemicals needed for clotting is absent from the blood.

THE FUTURE OF BLOOD

Your body is constantly renewing your blood. Even if it's not lost through a leaky vessel, a red cell lasts only around three or four months before it's recycled. In fact, your body has replaced your entire blood supply many times over in your lifetime.

As we've learned more about blood and how it works, we've found ways to help the body keep the blood it has. One drug, erythropoietin, actually stimulates your body's bone marrow to make blood faster. Some scalpels, those that use lasers or heat, can cut with little or no bleeding, sealing vessels as quickly as they open them.

But far beyond these developments lies the promise of artificial blood itself. Blood transfusions have been part of medicine for centuries, but they are not without problems. Artificial blood can't do everything our own blood does, but it might temporarily replace lost or damaged blood by carrying oxygen from lungs to cells. Hemoglobin-based oxygen carriers (HBOCs) are artificial bloods that use hemoglobin in artificial cells. Other blood replacements use chemicals called perfluorocarbons (PFCs) to carry oxygen. While both are still mostly experimental, they show just how far we've come in our understanding of blood and all it does.

Take a look at the next chapter to learn what scientists are doing to try to find matter that will be able to replicate what your body does routinely every day.

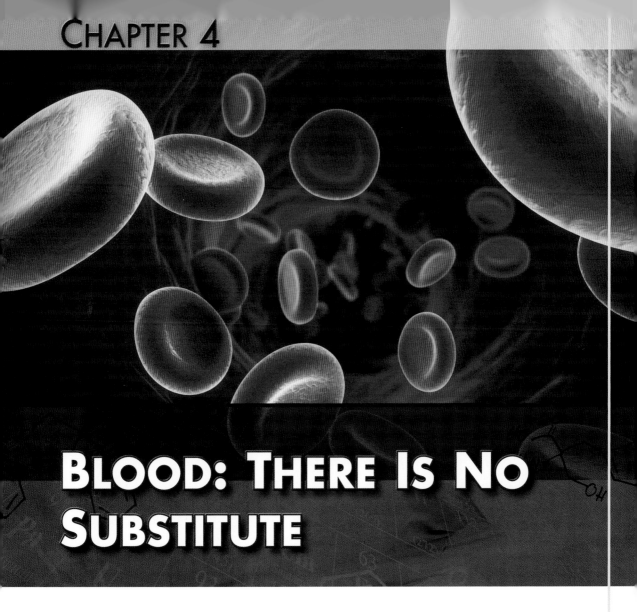

CHAPTER 4

BLOOD: THERE IS NO SUBSTITUTE

The mythical witch Medea had a great recipe for artificial blood. It called for thousands of ingredients such as screech owl wings, water snake skins, crow eggs, stag livers, and werewolf innards. Medea's specially blended blood substitute was reportedly quite effective. She drained an elderly patient's tired, old blood and replaced it with a fresh batch of her brew. The gentleman's health and youthful vigor were "magically restored."

MHΔEIΔ

Medea, according to Greek mythology, was a sorceress, or a witch, who married Jason, the famous hero who found the golden fleece.

Medea's method is not prescribed by modern doctors. It's too drastic, too complicated, and, well, just a myth. However, Medea's myth does illustrate an important medical truth: some patients need a replenishment of blood. Some need blood during surgery. Some need to replace blood loss due to traumatic injury or hemorrhage. Some need an influx of healthy blood to relieve the symptoms of disorders like hemophilia or anemia.

We all know there's no such thing as werewolf innards. But several real substances have been tried as substitutes for human blood. Salt water, animal bloods, ale, wine, and milk have all been pumped into human veins in hopes of finding a stand-in for blood. None of these substances was satisfactory. To date, the only acceptable replacement for human blood is more human blood.

THE NEED FOR A BLOOD STAND-IN

Human blood is given to patients who need it via blood transfusions. A blood transfusion is a medical procedure that transfers a unit of blood from one person (a donor) to another (a recipient). Blood transfusions are usually well tolerated and safe. They've been used to save many lives and to improve the quality of many, many more. As a replacement for human blood, donated blood has been an unmatched success.

Yet even blood is limited as a substitute for blood. Any two people cannot necessarily share blood. Special care must be taken to match the blood types of a donor and a recipient. Donated blood must also be screened to guarantee it's free of transmittable diseases like HIV and hepatitis. Packets of human blood have a limited shelf life. Even with refrigeration, blood lasts only about a month. Donors are continually needed to replenish stores of blood. Sometimes there are too few donors. This is particularly true in remote areas, during natural disasters, and on battlefields. In such situations, the demand for donated blood can exceed the supply.

Blood drives are common, as hospitals everywhere have a need for fresh blood to help sick patients. Mobile trucks will park at a business and collect blood during blood drives.

These limitations are the reason why some researchers want to develop an artificial substitute for blood. It's a bit audacious to try to make an artificial blood that's better at replacing blood than blood. Given the track record, it isn't an easy thing to accomplish, either. Artificial blood must be able to do what blood can, but other liquids like milk, wine, and ale, can't. Artificial blood must have the ability to push oxygen around.

As you've already learned, blood has many functions, but its single most critical job is to move oxygen around the body. Blood picks up inhaled oxygen in the lungs and takes it through the circulatory system. Blood drops off oxygen at the body's various organs and tissues. The importance of blood's oxygen delivery service cannot be overstated. If organs and tissues don't get enough oxygen, they cannot work properly. If organs and tissues are deprived of oxygen for too long, they cease to function and die.

Blood is able to move oxygen because of hemoglobin.

This image shows hemoglobin, which is the oxygen-carrying part of the red blood cells.

WILL HEMOGLOBIN DO THE JOB?

As you know, hemoglobin is a protein, and it is the component of blood that catches and releases oxygen. Hemoglobin grabs oxygen where there's a lot of it, like in the lungs. Hemoglobin lets go of oxygen where there isn't much of it, like in hard-working organs and tissues. Milk, like blood, has lots of protein. But milk cannot substitute for blood because milk doesn't have hemoglobin.

So why not give patients who need blood a whopping injection of hemoglobin? The reason is that hemoglobin does not float loose in the bloodstream. Hemoglobin is kept inside red blood cells. When red blood cells occasionally burst, the hemoglobin they release is broken up by the liver. This is part of the body's natural

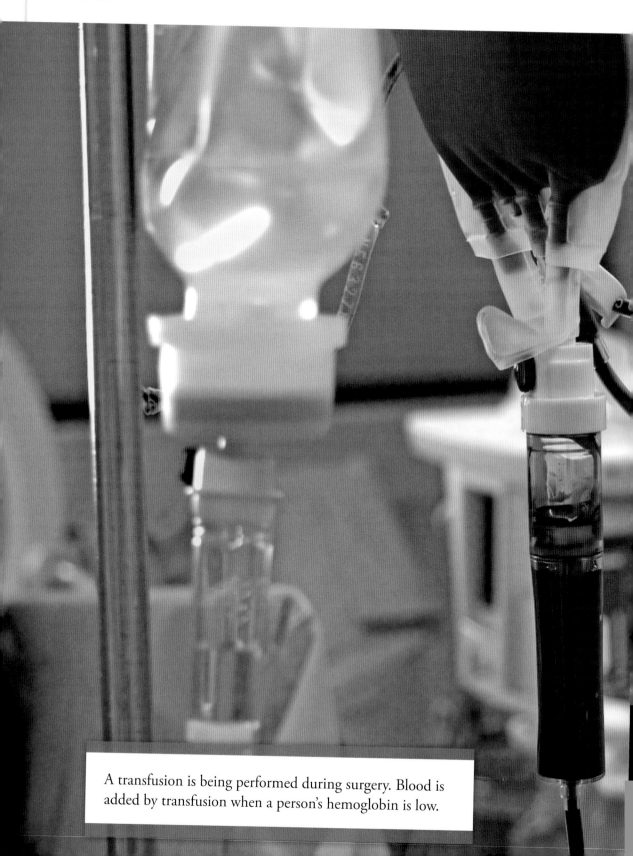

A transfusion is being performed during surgery. Blood is added by transfusion when a person's hemoglobin is low.

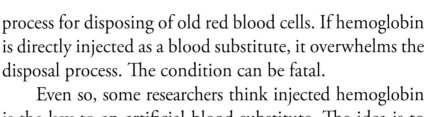

process for disposing of old red blood cells. If hemoglobin is directly injected as a blood substitute, it overwhelms the disposal process. The condition can be fatal.

Even so, some researchers think injected hemoglobin is the key to an artificial blood substitute. The idea is to alter the hemoglobin so that the liver doesn't break it up. The hemoglobin used in these experiments comes from cow's blood or from donated human blood that's past its expiration date. The hemoglobin is altered in one of two ways: a few hemoglobin proteins are joined together to make a multi-hemoglobin polymer, or small guard units are attached to hemoglobin. This is like building the protein a suit of armor.

Artificial hemoglobin was tested in human patients. Unfortunately, there were problems. The altered protein was associated with an increased risk of heart attack and death. It was argued that artificial hemoglobin could still be used to rescue critically injured patients who might otherwise die without immediate blood replacement. Such patients, however, are not in a position to give informed consent for an experimental procedure. They cannot judge for themselves whether they want to risk using artificial hemoglobin. The US Food and Drug Administration (FDA) has decided that, at least for the time being, no artificial hemoglobin will be given to human patients.

Future improvements to artificial hemoglobin may reduce the risk. Artificial hemoglobin may eventually be a useful blood substitute. As with any new drug or medical procedure, a balance must be struck between effective treatment and potentially harmful side effects.

The benefits of an artificial blood substitute based on hemoglobin would be many. Blood type matching and disease screening would be unnecessary. Blood substitute could be mass-produced and stored indefinitely. There would be plenty of artificial blood on hand for any, and every, emergency.

LET RED BLOOD CELLS DO IT

Rather than make artificial blood, it may become possible to make blood artificially. Two different methods for doing so are being developed.

Erythropoietin (EPO) is a hormone released by the kidneys that controls the production of red blood cells. The hormone can now be manufactured from the bit of human DNA that has the encoded instructions for making it. Erythropoietin stimulates bone marrow to generate red blood cells. Patients whose bones are artificially encouraged to make more blood need fewer transfusions of donated blood. Erythropoietin therapy may prove beneficial to individuals who suffer from chronic kidney disease or anemia caused by blood disorders or chemotherapy.

Hematopoietic stem cells are special cells found in the marrow of adult bones. These cells are capable of transforming into mature red blood cells. Researchers are looking for ways to collect and grow these cells in batches. Someday, blood made artificially by the batch may supplement the supply of blood from donations.

Erythropoietin and hematopoietic stem cells may make artificial hemoglobin unnecessary. Brand-spanking-new red blood cells can make plenty of natural hemoglobin all by themselves.

ARTIFICIAL BLOOD MEETS LIQUID BREATHING

Blood isn't the only fluid that can carry oxygen. Perfluorocarbons are man-made liquids that are able to dissolve a lot of oxygen gas. In 1966, a few dedicated mice at the University of Cincinnati proved it was possible to "breathe" perfluorocarbons. The mice survived for up to an hour while submerged in oxygen-enriched liquid.

Where the mice led, science fiction followed. It was speculated that divers and astronauts of the future might benefit from perfluorocarbon technology. Two films, James Cameron's *The Abyss* and Brian De Palma's *Mission to Mars*, depicted Hollywood-style liquid breathing. In *The Abyss*, a stunt rat was actually plunged into a container of "oxygenated fluorocarbon emulsion" as an authentic demonstration.

No major movie has featured perfluorocarbons in the role of artificial blood. But in real life, researchers are trying exactly that. They're developing ways to substitute perfluorocarbons for human blood. There are some technical difficulties. Perfluorocarbons don't stay in the human body very long, and some patients receiving perfluorocarbon treatments have reported flu-like symptoms. If these problems are resolved, perfluorocarbons may be used as artificial blood. Stay tuned to science developments (and theaters) near you.

For the time being, the only help for patients who need blood comes from some very important individuals. These individuals are certainly not witches or werewolves. They are not (yet) the researchers working to come up with an artificial blood substitute. They are the generous donors who contribute blood to their local blood banks. For them, there also is no substitute.

GLOSSARY

anemia A deficiency in the oxygen-carrying component of the blood.

artery A muscular, elastic tube that carries blood away from the heart.

audacious Fearlessly daring.

bone marrow The jelly-like interior core of long bones such as the femur and humerus, which contains developing blood cells of all types.

capillary One of the fine, branching blood vessels that form a network between the arteries and the veins.

carbon dioxide A gas composed of one carbon atom attached to two oxygen atoms—a byproduct of energy production in all cells.

carbon monoxide A gas composed of one atom of carbon attached to one atom of oxygen—a byproduct of incomplete burning of carbon-based fuels, caused by lack of enough oxygen. Almost all routine burning of fuel produces incomplete combustion.

chamber A room or space.

heme ring A circular structure called a porphyrin ring, built of molecules containing carbon and at least one other type of atom, such as sulfur, nitrogen, or oxygen, with iron at the center.

hemophilia Any of several hereditary disorders in which the blood fails to clot normally.

stem cell A type of cell that still has the ability to differentiate into a cell with a specialized function.

valve A device that controls the flow of fluids through a tube.

vein A muscular, elastic tube that carries oxygen-poor blood toward the heart.

BOOKS

Canavan, Thomas. *Fit and Healthy: Heart, Lungs, and Hormones.* New York, NY: PowerKids Press, 2015.

Gold, John C. *Learning About the Circulatory and Lymphatic Systems.* Berkeley Heights, NJ: Enslow Publishers, 2013.

Kingston, Anna, and Jennifer Viegas. *The Heart in 3D.* New York, NY: Rosen Central, 2015.

Mason, Paul. *Your Hardworking Heart and Spectacular Circulatory System.* New York, NY: Crabtree Publishing, 2015.

Yount, Lisa. *William Harvey: Genius Discoverer of Blood Circulation.* Berkeley Heights, NJ: Enslow Publishers, 2015.

WEBSITES

Discovery Kids: Your Cardiovascular System
discoverykids.com/articles/your-cardiovascular-system
Learn more facts about the cardiovascular system.

National Geographic: Heart
science.nationalgeographic.com/science/health-and-human-body/human-body/heart-article
View interactive diagrams that illustrate the functions and anatomy of a healthy heart, as well as what happens during a heart attack.

TeensHealth: Heart and Circulatory System
kidshealth.org/en/teens/heart.html
Read more information about the heart and circulatory system.

INDEX

A
adrenaline, 16
arteries, 5, 9, 10, 13, 18
atria, 5

B
blood
    artificial, 34, 39, 43–44, 45
    creation of, 13, 17
    functions of, 11–15, 29, 39
    makeup of, 11–13
blood transfusions, 34, 37–38
blushing, 15–16

C
capillaries, 18, 20–21, 31
carbon dioxide, 11, 13, 21, 31
carbon monoxide, 21–23

E
erythropoietin, 34, 44

F
fibrin, 33

G
Galen, 6–8
globins, 19, 25

H
Harvey, William, 8–10, 11
heart, chambers of, 5
hematopoietic stem cells, 44
heme ring, 19, 23
hemoglobin, 13, 17, 19–21, 23,
    25–27, 34, 39, 41–44

hemoglobin-based oxygen
    carriers, 34
hemophilia, 33, 37

I
iron, 19, 20, 21, 23

L
lungs, 8, 9, 11, 13, 18, 20, 21,
    23, 31, 34, 39, 41

O
oxygen, 11, 13, 15, 17–22, 27,
    30, 31, 34, 39, 41, 45

P
perfluorocarbons, 34, 45
plasma, 11
platelets, 13, 30, 33

R
red blood cells, 13, 17, 18, 19,
    20, 23, 27, 30, 31, 34, 41,
    43, 44

S
sickle cell trait, 25–27

V
valves, 5, 10
veins, 4, 5, 6, 9, 10, 18
ventricles, 5

W
white blood cells, 13, 30, 31